≈ Introduction

Wraps and rolls are fast catching up in popularity, not just at street-side vendors and fast food stalls but even at the food courts of some of the most up-market malls in India. One of the oldest forms of fast-food, wraps are easy to make and serve absolutely no fuss! You do not have to create a large spread; at the same time you can take the liberty to mix-and-match ingredients from different cuisines and simply wrap them up in a *roti*!

Earlier in India, people used to be content with creating simple rolls using left-over *rotis* filled with *bhaji* and a*chaar*, or occasionally a salad garnished with grated cheese. Overseas, wraps and rolls were predominantly associated with the ever-so-popular Burrito. However, with the rise in the demand for quick-eats, people have started experimenting with their own regional cuisines and creating innovative wraps and rolls.

Keeping in mind the needs of the modern, fast-paced world where no one has the time to sit down and have complete meals, we have come up with a cookbook of **"WRAPS AND ROLLS"** that blends the grandeur of Indian cuisine with the sophistication of international gourmet food.

We start with **"Indian Wraps & Rolls"** where you will find a wide variety of starters and sauces from the different regions of India wrapped up in the humble *roti* to make exotic dishes! Pahadi Paneer Tikka Wrap, page 8, and Makhmali Paneer Tikka Roll, page 22, bring us close to the soil of Punjab, whereas the royal Vegetable Shikampuri Kebab Roll page 26, transports us back to the glorious Moghul era when Hyderabadi cuisine was in full bloom.

The **"International Wraps & Rolls"** section has been inspired as much by the exotic Asian flavours as by the gypsy-like feel of Mexican cuisine. Herbed Cottage Cheese Wrap, page 44, and Asparagus and Baby Corn Wrap, page 52, have a classy continental feel, whereas the Mushroom Schezuan Wrap, page 48, and the Thai Satay Paneer Wrap page 56, takes us all the way to the heart of China.

We've not forgotten our health-conscious readers either. The **"Healthy Wraps & Rolls"** section is a selection of nutritious rolls that are equally delicious. Try out the Hara Bhara Tikki Roll, page 64, and the Spinach Tahini Wrap, page 86.

The recipes have also been labelled as bland, spicy and double spicy, as is usually done on the menu of a restaurant or at the wraps and rolls corner. This makes it easy for you to wade through the recipes and take your pick!

Get set to expand your cooking skills (and eating options!) with these 39 easy-to-follow recipes. Explore the method of making a basic *roti*, page 91, along with various ways in which you call fill up the ubiquitous *roti* with fillings from across the globe! You'll enjoy creating these wraps for your friends and family, as a complete meal or as the star attraction of a wraps and rolls party!

Happy Cooking!

Regards

Tarla Dalal

≈ Index ≈

≈ Indian Wraps & Rolls

- Pahadi Paneer Tikka Wrap................. 8
- Khumbh Curry Wrap...................... 10
- Paneer Tikka Kathi Roll.................... 12
- Rajma Tikki Wrap.......................... 14
- Makhani Paneer Tikka Roll 16
- Tandoori Aloo Wrap 18
- Pindi Chole Roll 20
- Makhmali Paneer Tikka Wrap.......... 22
- Aloo Frankie................................. 24
- Vegetable Shikampuri Kebab Roll..... 26
- Paneer-N-Cheese Roll 28
- Achaari Aloo Roll 30
- Cheesy Khada Bhaji Wrap 32

≈ International Wraps & Rolls

- Burritos 36
- Vegetable Manchurian Roll.................... 38
- Vegetable and Noodle Wrap 40
- Mexican Tortilla Wrap.......................... 42
- Herbed Cottage Cheese Wrap 44
- Cheese Corn Balls Wrap....................... 46
- Mushroom Schezuan Wrap 48
- Lebanese Roll 50
- Asparagus and Baby Corn Wrap 52
- Mexican Kebab Roll............................. 54
- Thai Satay Paneer Wrap 56
- Potato Cream Cheese Roll..................... 58
- Chilli Paneer Wrap.............................. 60

 ∥ - Spicy   ∥ - Double Spicy

Healthy Wraps & Rolls

Hara Bhara Tikki Roll...................... 64

Mixed Sprouts Wrap 66

Chick Pea and Soya Tikki Roll.......... 68

Whole Wheat Salad Wrap 70

Mint and Masoor Roll 72

Paneer Khurchan Roll 74

Stir-Fry Wrap 76

Makai Khumbh Jalfrazie Roll 78

Chatpata Rajma Roll 80

Herbed Yoghurt Corn Cake Wrap 82

Honeyed Tofu and Pepper Roll 84

Spinach Tahini Wrap........................ 86

Paneer Tikki Salsa Wrap 88

Basic Recipes

Roti... 90

Spinach Roti 90

Soya Roti 90

Tortillas.. 90

Sweet and Sour Sauce 92

Healthy Green Chutney.............. 92

Schezuan Sauce........................... 93

Chilli-Garlic Chutney 93

Sour Cream 94

Garlic-Tomato Chutney............... 94

Stir-Fried Rice 95

Low Fat Curds 95

Low-Fat Paneer 96

Low-Cal Mayonnaise 96

~Indian Wraps & Rolls~

Indian cuisine has an enduring charm, and not surprisingly, it has its share of die-hard fans. This section is especially for such people! Enjoy this impressive selection of mouth-watering rolls inspired by cuisines from different parts of the country.

A variety of *paneer*-based rolls such as **Pahadi Paneer Tikka Wrap, page 8, Makhani Paneer Tikka Roll, page 16,** and **Paneer-N-Cheese Roll, page 28,** have been marinated in some of the most delicious marinades to give each *paneer*-based wrap a whole new character and identity of its own. An equally sumptuous selection of kebab-based rolls has been created using authentic recipes from the Moghul era, like the **Vegetable Shikampuri Kebab Roll, page 26,** and straight from the land of five rivers, Punjab, you have the **Rajma Tikki Wrap, page 14** and the **Pindi Chole Roll, page 20.**

I have tried to give a unique twist to some snacks like *pav bhaji* by creating the utterly yummy **Cheesy Khada Bhaji Wrap, page 32.** All these wraps have been topped with sauces that beautifully complement and enhance the flavours of these wraps. To further enhance the texture and mellow down the flavour, we have added raw salads to the wraps.

≈ Pahadi Paneer Tikka Wrap ≈

Paneer and onions marinated in a delectable curd and mint based marinade, makes this an irresistible tikka! The key to ensuring that the marinade doesn't slide off the tikkas is to use hung curds and not miss out use of cornflour. Wrap the tikkas with a handful of onion rings sprinkled with chaat masala for a simple yet delicious combo!

PREPARATION TIME : 20 MINUTES.   COOKING TIME : 6 TO 8 MINUTES.   MAKES 4 WRAPS.

For the *pahadi* marinade
1 cup chopped mint leaves (*phudina*)
½ cup chopped coriander (*dhania*)
3 tbsp hung curds (*dahi*)
1 tsp cumin seeds (*jeera*)
2 green chillies, roughly chopped
1 tsp lemon juice
Salt to taste
1 tbsp cornflour
1 tbsp fresh cream

For the *paneer tikkas*
16 pieces *paneer* (cottage cheese), cut into 25 mm. (1") cubes
16 pieces capsicum, cut into 25 mm. (1") cubes
16 pieces onions, cut into 25 mm. (1") cubes
1 tbsp oil for cooking

Other ingredients
1 cup onion rings
Chaat masala to taste
4 *rotis*, page 90

For the *pahadi* marinade
1. Combine all the ingredients, except the cornflour and cream, and blend in a mixer to a smooth paste, without using water.
2. Add the cornflour and cream, mix well and keep aside.

For the *paneer tikkas*
1. Combine the *paneer* cubes, capsicum cubes, onion cubes and half the marinade in a bowl and toss gently. Keep aside to marinate for 10 minutes.
2. On a satay stick, arrange 4 pieces each of *paneer*, capsicum and onion cubes alternatively. Repeat with the remaining ingredients to make 3 more satays.
3. Heat a non-stick *tava* (griddle) and cook the satays on a medium flame using oil till the *paneer* is light brown in colour from all sides. Keep aside.

How to proceed
1. Combine the onions rings with *chaat masala* in a bowl, mix well and keep aside.
2. Place a *roti* on a clean dry surface and slide the *paneer tikkas* from 1 satay stick in a row in the centre of the *roti*, gently using a knife.
3. Arrange ¼ cup of onion rings over the *paneer tikkas*.
4. Finally spread ¼th of the remaining *pahadi* marinade over it and roll it up tightly.
5. Repeat with the remaining ingredients to make 3 more wraps.
6. Wrap a tissue paper around each wrap and serve immediately.

~ Khumbh Curry Wrap ~

A must-try for mushroom lovers! I really like mushrooms as it easily takes on earthy flavours of curry powder and kasuri methi. Succulent mushrooms when rolled up with onions and carrots makes this a heavenly treat. What's more! It is totally healthy and light on calories.

PREPARATION TIME : 15 MINUTES.   COOKING TIME : 7 TO 8 MINUTES.   MAKES 4 WRAPS.

For the mushroom *curry* stuffing
1 tbsp oil
1 tbsp ginger-garlic (*adrak-lehsun*) paste
1 cup finely chopped onions
1 cup finely chopped tomatoes
3 tbsp chilli-garlic *chutney*, page 93
1 tbsp dried fenugreek leaves (*kasuri methi*)
½ tsp *curry* powder
2 cups mushrooms (*khumbh*), cut into quarters and blanched
Salt to taste

Other ingredients
1 cup onion rings
1 cup grated carrots
Chaat masala to taste
4 *rotis*, page 90

For the mushroom *curry* stuffing
1. Heat the oil in a broad pan, add the ginger-garlic paste and onions and sauté on a medium flame till the onions turn translucent.
2. Add the tomatoes, chilli-garlic *chutney*, dried fenugreek leaves and *curry* powder and sauté on a medium flame for another 2 to 3 minutes.
3. Add the mushrooms and salt, mix gently and cook on a medium flame for a minute, while stirring continuously. Keep aside.

How to proceed
1. Combine the onion rings, carrots and *chaat masala* in a bowl, mix gently and keep aside.
2. Place a *roti* on a clean dry surface and place ¼th of the stuffing in a row in the centre of the *roti*.
3. Arrange ¼th of the onion-carrot mixture over the stuffing and roll it up tightly.
4. Repeat with the remaining ingredients to make 3 more wraps.
5. Wrap a tissue paper around each wrap and serve immediately.

≈ Paneer Tikka Kathi Roll ≈

What an amazing roll this is! Folks will keep popping into your kitchen even as you make this treat, lured by the aroma of paneer, onions and capsicum tossed in a spicy marinade. This all-time favourite and time-tested recipe will never fail you.

PREPARATION TIME : 15 MINUTES.   COOKING TIME : 6 TO 8 MINUTES.   MAKES 4 ROLLS.

To be mixed together into a marinade
½ cup curds (dahi)
1½ tsp chilli powder
¼ tsp turmeric powder (haldi)
¾ tsp ginger (adrak) paste
½ tsp garlic (lehsun) paste
½ tsp besan (Bengal gram flour)
¾ tsp chaat masala
½ tsp dried fenugreek leaves (kasuri methi)
¾ tsp garam masala
Salt to taste

For the paneer tikka filling
16 pieces paneer (cottage cheese), cut into 25 mm. (1") cubes
16 pieces onions, cut into 25 mm. (1") cubes
16 pieces capsicum, cut into 25 mm. (1") cubes
1 tbsp oil for cooking

Other ingredients
1 cup onion rings
Chaat masala to taste
4 rotis, page 90

For the paneer tikkas
1. Combine the paneer cubes, onion cubes, capsicum cubes and the marinade in a bowl and toss gently. Keep aside to marinate for 10 minutes.
2. On a satay stick, arrange 4 pieces each of paneer, onion and capsicum cubes alternatively. Repeat with the remaining ingredients to make 3 more satays.
3. Heat a non-stick tava (griddle) and cook the satays on a medium flame using oil till the paneer is light brown in colour from all sides. Keep aside.

How to proceed
1. Combine the onions rings with chaat masala in a bowl, mix well and keep aside.
2. Place a roti on a clean dry surface and slide the paneer tikkas from 1 satay stick in a row in the centre of the roti, gently using a knife.
3. Arrange ¼ cup of onion rings over the paneer tikkas and roll it up tightly.
4. Repeat with the remaining ingredients to make 3 more rolls.
5. Wrap a tissue paper around each roll and serve immediately.

≈ Rajma Tikki Wrap ≈

A traditional Punjabi starter transforms into an exotic and innovative wrap when combined with fresh veggies like spring onion whites, lettuce and carrots. The addition of mayonnaise binds the flavours of this wrap, and enhances its appeal. To avoid the rajma tikkis from turning soggy, ensure that you drain the cooked rajma and leave it aside in the sieve for at least five minutes, so they become completely dry. Also, don't forget to coat the tikkis with cornflour.

PREPARATION TIME : 20 MINUTES.   COOKING TIME : 20 MINUTES.   MAKES 4 WRAPS.

For the *rajma tikkis*
¾ cup sliced onions
2 tbsp *ghee*
2 tbsp finely chopped ginger (*adrak*)
1½ tsp finely chopped green chillies
¼ tsp turmeric powder (*haldi*)
1 cup soaked and boiled *rajma* (kidney beans), lightly mashed
½ cup boiled, peeled and mashed potatoes
¼ cup crumbled *paneer* (*cottage cheese*)
2 tbsp chopped coriander (*dhania*)
¾ tsp *garam masala*
Salt to taste
3 tbsp cornflour
Cornflour for coating
Oil for deep-frying

Other ingredients
½ cup grated carrots
½ cup finely chopped spring onion whites
Chaat masala to taste
4 *rotis*, page 90
1 cup lettuce, torn into pieces
6 tbsp mayonnaise

For the *rajma tikkis*
1. Heat the oil in a *kadhai* and deep-fry the onions on a medium flame till they are golden brown in colour. Drain on absorbent paper and keep aside. Keep the *kadhai* aside to deep-fry the *tikkis* later.
2. Heat the ghee in a broad pan, add the ginger and green chillies and sauté for 30 seconds.

3. Add the turmeric powder, *rajma*, potatoes, *paneer*, fried onions, coriander, *garam masala* and salt, mix well and cook on a medium flame for 3 to 4 minutes, while stirring continuously.
4. Cool slightly, add the cornflour and mix well.
5. Divide the mixture into 8 equal portions and shape each portion into 50 mm. (2") oval flat *tikkis*.
6. Roll each *tikki in* cornflour in such a way that the *tikkis* are evenly coated from both the sides.
7. Heat the remaining oil in the same *kadhai* and deep-fry the *tikkis* on a medium flame till they are golden brown in colour from all the sides. Drain on absorbent paper and keep aside.

How to proceed
1. Combine the carrots, spring onion whites and *chaat masala* in a bowl, mix well and keep aside.
2. Place a *roti* on a clean dry surface and arrange ¼ cup of lettuce in a row in the centre of the *roti*.
3. Place 2 *tikkis* and arrange ¼th of the carrot-spring onion white mixture over it.
4. Finally spread 1½ tbsp of mayonnaise over it and roll it up tightly.
5. Repeat with the remaining ingredients to make 3 more wraps.
6. Wrap a tissue paper around each wrap and serve immediately.

≈ Makhani Paneer Tikka Roll ≈

Straight from the kitchens of Punjab, curd-marinated paneer topped with makhani sauce is perfectly complemented by the earthy spices and herbs, which are in turn mellowed with fresh cream! In addition to the authentic makhani sauce, this wrap also features salads and mayonnaise, which impart an interesting fusion touch to it.

PREPARATION TIME : 15 MINUTES.   COOKING TIME : 18 TO 20 MINUTES.   MAKES 4 ROLLS.

For the *Makhani* sauce
3 large tomatoes, roughly chopped
2 cloves (*laung / lavang*)
4 to 5 cashewnuts (*kaju*)
1 tbsp oil
1 tbsp butter
½ tsp cumin seeds (*jeera*)
2 tsp ginger-garlic (*adrak-lehsun*) paste
½ cup finely chopped onions
1 tsp chilli powder
3 tbsp fresh cream
¼ tsp *garam masala*
½ tsp dried fenugreek leaves (*kasuri methi*)
1 tsp tomato ketchup
1 tsp sugar
Salt to taste

For the *paneer tikkas*
16 pieces *paneer* (cottage cheese), cut into 25 mm. (1") cubes
16 pieces onions, cut into 25 mm. (1") cubes
16 pieces capsicum, cut into 25 mm. (1") cubes
1 tbsp oil for cooking

To be mixed together into a marinade
1 cup fresh curds (*dahi*)
2 tsp ginger-garlic (*adrak-lehsun*) paste
½ tsp crushed carom seeds (*ajwain*)
½ tsp roasted and crushed dried fenugreek leaves (*kasuri methi*)
1 tbsp chilli-garlic *chutney*, page 93

2 tsp cornflour
Salt to taste

Other ingredients
2 cups shredded cabbage
1 cup grated carrots
Chaat masala to taste
4 *rotis*, page 90

For the *Makhani* sauce
1. Combine the tomatoes, cloves, cashewnuts and oil with ¼ cup of water and blend in a mixer to a smooth purée.
2. Strain the purée using a strainer and keep aside.
3. Melt the butter in a broad pan and add the cumin seeds.
4. When the seeds crackle, add the ginger-garlic paste and sauté for a few seconds.
5. Add the onions and sauté on a medium flame till they turn translucent.
6. Add the strained tomato purée, chilli powder, fresh cream, *garam masala*, dried fenugreek leaves, tomato ketchup, sugar and salt, mix well and bring to boil. Keep aside to cool.
7. Add ¼ cup of water and blend in a mixer to a smooth paste. Keep aside.

For the *paneer tikkas*
1. Combine the *paneer* cubes, onion cubes, capsicum cubes and the marinade in a bowl and toss gently. Keep aside to marinate for 10 minutes.

≈ **16** ≈

2. On a satay stick, arrange 4 pieces each of *paneer*, capsicum and onion cubes alternatively. Repeat with the remaining ingredients to make 3 more satays.

3. Heat a non-stick *tava* (griddle) and cook the satays on a medium flame using oil till the *paneer* is light brown in colour from all sides. Keep aside.

How to proceed

1. Combine the cabbage, carrots and *chaat masala* in a bowl, mix well and keep aside.

2. Place a *roti* on a clean dry surface and slide the *paneer tikkas* from 1 satay stick in a row in the centre on the *roti*, gently using a knife.

3. Arrange ¼th of the cabbage-carrot mixture over the *paneer tikkas*.

4. Finally spread ¼th of the *Makhani* sauce and over it and roll it up tightly.

5. Repeat with the remaining ingredients to make 3 more rolls.

6. Wrap a tissue paper around each roll and serve immediately.

≈ Tandoori Aloo Wrap ≈

Baby potatoes tossed in a spicy paste and then wrapped up with a flavoured curd dressing – let's see if you can say 'no' to this! The mildness of curds complements the spicy Tandoori aloo in this lip-smacking wrap! When making for kids reduce the chilli-garlic chutney and instead increase the amount of fresh cream used in this recipe.

PREPARATION TIME : 20 MINUTES.   COOKING TIME : 15 MINUTES.   MAKES 4 WRAPS.

To be mixed together into a paste
1½ tbsp chilli-garlic *chutney*, page 93
2 tsp ginger *(adrak)* paste
3 tsp coriander-cumin seeds *(dhania-jeera)* powder

For the *tandoori aloo* stuffing
24 baby potatoes, boiled and peeled, refer handy tip
1 tbsp oil
1 tsp dried fenugreek leaves *(kasuri methi)*
2 tbsp fresh cream
Salt to taste
1 tbsp finely chopped coriander *(dhania)*

To be mixed together into a curd dressing
½ cup fresh curds *(dahi)*
4 spring onions, finely chopped
2 cloves garlic *(lehsun)*, finely chopped
½ tsp cumin seeds *(jeera)* powder
½ tsp finely chopped green chillies
1 tbsp milk
A pinch sugar
Salt to taste

Other ingredients
1 cup shredded cabbage
1 cup grated carrots
Chaat masala to taste
4 spinach *rotis,* page 90

For the *tandoori aloo* stuffing
1. Cut the baby potatoes into halves and keep aside.
2. Heat the oil in a broad pan, add the prepared paste and sauté for 2 minutes.
3. Add the dried fenugreek leaves and cook for another minute.
4. Add the potatoes, fresh cream, salt and coriander, mix well and cook on a medium flame for 2 to 3 minutes. Keep aside.

How to proceed
1. Combine the cabbage, carrots and *chaat masala* in a bowl, mix well and keep aside.
2. Place a spinach *roti* on a clean dry surface and place ¼th of the *tandoori aloo* stuffing in a row in the centre of the *roti.*
3. Arrange ¼th of the cabbage-carrot mixture over the stuffing.
4. Finally spread ¼th of the curd dressing over it and roll it up tightly.
5. Repeat with the remaining ingredients to make 3 more wraps.
6. Wrap a tissue paper around each wrap and serve immediately.

Handy tip : To induce the baby potatoes to absorb the flavours of the paste, scrub the baby potatoes roughly and prick all over gently with a fork. Boil a vesselful of water with a little salt and cook the baby potatoes in it till done. Peel and use as per the recipe.

≈ Pindi Chole Roll ≈

Each mouthful of this wrap feels so complete, and is so satiating! Hmmm... Pindi chole topped with gajar ka achaar and onion rings and rolled up in a simple roti, this makes a wholesome snack by itself. A two-minute wrap when you have leftover chole in the refrigerator!

PREPARATION TIME : 20 MINUTES.   COOKING TIME : 30 MINUTES.   MAKES 4 ROLLS.   SOAKING TIME : 6 TO 8 HOURS.

For the *pindi chole* stuffing
¾ cup *kabuli chana* (chick peas)
1½ tsp *chana dal* (split Bengal gram)
1 black cardamom (*badi elaichi*)
25 mm. (1") stick cinnamon (*dalchini*)
1 teabag
4 tbsp oil
¾ cup chopped onions
1½ tsp pomegranate (*anardana*) powder
¾ cup chopped tomatoes
1 tsp chopped ginger (*adrak*)
1½ tsp chopped green chillies
1 tsp coriander (*dhania*) powder
½ tsp chilli powder
½ tsp *garam masala*
¾ tsp *chana masala*
Salt to taste

Other ingredients
1 cup onion rings
Chaat masala to taste
4 *rotis*, page 90
4 tsp *gajar ka achaar* (readily available in the market)
4 tbsp finely chopped coriander (*dhania*)

For the *pindi chole* stuffing
1. Wash and soak the *kabuli chana* and *chana dal* for 6 to 8 hours or overnight.
2. Drain, wash again, add 1½ cups of water, big cardamom, cinnamon and teabag and pressure cook on a high flame for 3 whistles.
3. Lower the flame and pressure cook for another 3 whistles.

4. Allow the steam to escape before opening the lid.
5. Discard the tea bag and strain the *kabuli chana*.
6. Heat the oil in a *kadhai*, add the onions and sauté till they turn translucent.
7. Add the pomegranate powder and sauté on a medium flame till the onions turn dark brown.
8. Add the tomatoes, ginger and green chillies and sauté on a medium flame for another 3 to 4 minutes.
9. Add the coriander powder, chilli powder and *garam masala* and cook on a medium flame for 4 to 5 minutes or till the tomatoes are cooked and the mixture leaves oil.
10. Add the cooked *kabuli chana*, *chana masala*, 2 tbsp of water and salt and mix well.
11. Cook on a medium flame for another 3 to 4 minutes till the liquid dries up. Keep aside.

How to proceed
1. Combine the onion rings with *chaat masala* in a bowl, mix well and keep aside.
2. Place a *roti* on a clean dry surface and place ¼th of the *chole* in a row in the centre of the *roti*.
3. Arrange ¼ cup of onion rings and spread 1 tsp of *gajar ka achaar* over it.
4. Finally sprinkle 1 tbsp of coriander over it and roll it up tightly.
5. Repeat with the remaining ingredients to make 3 more rolls.
6. Wrap a tissue paper around each roll and serve immediately.

≈ Makhmali Paneer Tikka Wrap ≈

Makhmali - the name says it all! Paneer marinated in this divine Makhmali marinade is so succulent and soft that it melts in your mouth. The pahadi marinade complements the delicate flavours of the tikka so well that it will definitely steal the show at your parties.

PREPARATION TIME : 15 MINUTES.   COOKING TIME : 6 TO 8 MINUTES.   MAKES 4 WRAPS.

To be mixed together into *Makhmali* marinade
¾ cup thick fresh hung curds (*dahi*)
¼ cup cheese spread
1 tsp green chilli paste
2 tbsp cashewnut (*kaju*) powder
½ tsp *garam masala*
Salt to taste

For the *paneer tikkas*
24 pieces *paneer* (cottage cheese), cut into 25 mm. (1") cubes
1 tbsp oil for cooking

Other ingredients
1 cup onion rings
1 cup shredded cabbage
½ cup grated carrots
Chaat masala to taste
4 tbsp finely chopped mint leaves (*phudina*)
4 spinach *rotis*, page 90
6 tbsp *pahadi* marinade, page 8

For the *paneer tikkas*
1. Combine the *paneer* cubes and half the *Makhmali* marinade in a bowl and toss gently. Keep aside to marinate for 10 minutes.
2. On a satay stick, arrange 6 pieces of *paneer* cubes. Repeat with the remaining ingredients to make 3 more satays.
3. Heat a non-stick *tava* (griddle) and cook the satays on a medium flame using oil till the *paneer* is light brown in colour from all sides. Keep aside.

How to proceed
1. Combine the onion rings, cabbage, carrots and *chaat masala* in a bowl, mix well and keep aside.
2. Roll each *paneer tikka* satay in the mint leaves till they are evenly coated from all sides.
3. Place a spinach *roti* on a clean dry surface and slide the *paneer tikkas* from 1 satay stick in a row in the centre of the *roti*, gently using a knife.
4. Arrange ¼th of the onion, cabbage and carrot mixture over the *paneer tikkas*.
5. Finally spread ¼th of the remaining *Makhmali* marinade and 1½ tbsp of *pahadi* marinade over it and roll it up tightly.
6. Repeat with the remaining ingredients to make 3 more wraps.
7. Wrap a tissue paper around each wrap and serve immediately.

~ Aloo Frankie ~

The Aloo Frankie truly needs no introduction! This one is an authentic recipe that simply never fails you. With a balance of flavours ranging from tangy to spicy it will be enjoyed by young and old alike.

PREPARATION TIME : 30 MINUTES.   COOKING TIME : 20 MINUTES.   MAKES 4 FRANKIES.

For the stuffing
1½ tbsp oil/butter
1 tsp ginger-garlic *(adrak-lehsun)* paste
1¾ cups boiled, peeled and mashed potatoes
¾ tsp chilli powder
1 tsp *garam masala*
½ tsp *chaat masala* (optional)
1 tbsp finely chopped coriander *(dhania)*
Salt to taste

To be mixed into *masala* water
1 tsp dried mango powder *(amchur)*
½ tsp chilli powder
¼ tsp *garam masala*
Salt to taste
3 tbsp water

To be mixed into onion *masala* mixture
½ cup finely chopped onions
¾ tsp chilli powder
½ tsp dry mango powder *(amchur)*
Salt to taste

Other ingredients
4 *rotis*, page 90
4 tsp green chillies in vinegar, refer handy tip

For the stuffing
1. Heat the oil/butter in a *kadhai,* add the ginger-garlic paste and sauté on a medium flame for a few seconds.
2. Add the potatoes, chilli powder, *garam masala, chaat masala,* coriander and salt, mix well and sauté for another 2 minutes. Keep aside.

How to proceed
1. Place a *roti* on a clean dry surface and spread ¼th of the potato stuffing in a row in the centre of the *roti.*
2. Drizzle ¼th of the *masala* water and 1 tsp of chillies in the vinegar evenly over it.
3. Sprinkle ¼th of the onion *masala* mixture on it and roll it up tightly.
4. Repeat with the remaining ingredients to make 3 more *frankies.*
5. Wrap a tissue paper around each *frankie* and serve immediately.

Handy tip: For chillies in vinegar, mix 3 tsp of white vinegar with 1 tsp finely chopped green chillies.

～ Vegetable Shikampuri Kebab Roll ～

An exquisite vegetarian variant of the famous Hyderabadi Shikampuri kebabs, these have been prepared with a fine blend of mashed vegetables, khoya and aromatic spices. Enticingly topped with Makhani sauce, this kebab roll will make you feel like royalty.

PREPARATION TIME : 20 MINUTES.   COOKING TIME : 15 TO 20 MINUTES.   MAKES 4 ROLLS.

For the *Shikampuri kebab*
2 tbsp *ghee*
¾ cup finely chopped onions
1 tsp caraway seeds (*shahjeera*)
½ tsp finely chopped ginger (*adrak*)
1 tsp finely chopped green chillies
¼ tsp turmeric powder (*haldi*)
1 tsp chilli powder
¾ cup roughly chopped and parboiled mixed vegetables (carrots, cauliflower, green peas, French beans etc.)
¾ cup boiled, peeled and mashed potatoes
Salt to taste
2 tbsp chopped mint leaves (*phudina*)
2 tbsp finely chopped coriander (*dhania*)
¼ cup grated *paneer* (cottage cheese)
¼ cup *mava* (*khoya*)
¼ cup breadcrumbs
A pinch freshly ground pepper
½ tsp cardamom (*elaichi*) powder
4 tsp oil for cooking

Other ingredients
1 cup finely chopped onions
1 cup finely chopped tomatoes
Chaat masala to taste
4 *rotis*, page 90,
8 tbsp *Makhani* sauce, page 16

For the *Shikampuri kebab*
1. Heat 1 tbsp of ghee in a broad pan, add the onions and saute till they turn dark brown in colour. Remove and keep aside.

2. Heat the remaining 1 tbsp of ghee in the same pan and add the caraway seeds.
3. When the seeds crackle, add the ginger, green chillies, turmeric powder, chilli powder, mixed vegetables, potatoes and salt and mix well. Mash lightly using the back of a spoon and sauté for 2 to 3 minutes, while stirring continuously.
4. Add the mint leaves and coriander and sauté on a medium flame for another minute. Keep aside to cool.
5. Add the *paneer*, *mava*, breadcrumbs, browned onions, pepper and cardamom powder and mix well.
6. Divide the mixture into 8 equal portions and shape each portion into 50 mm. (2") oval flat *kebabs*.
7. Heat a non-stick *tava* (griddle) and cook each *kebab* using ½ tsp of oil till they are golden brown in colour from both the sides.
8. Drain on absorbent paper and keep aside.

How to proceed
1. Combine the onions, tomatoes and *chaat masala* in a bowl, mix well and keep aside.
2. Place a *roti* on a clean dry surface and place 2 *tikkis* in a row in the centre of the *roti*.
3. Arrange ¼th of the onion-tomato mixture over the *tikkis*.
4. Finally spread 2 tbsp of the *Makhani* sauce over it and roll it up tightly.
5. Repeat with the remaining ingredients to make 3 more rolls.
6. Wrap a tissue paper around each roll and serve immediately.

~ Paneer-N-Cheese Roll ~

The versatility of paneer never ceases to amaze me! Cooking the paneer in this lip-smacking marinade imparts a delicious feel to the wrap. The salads as well as the special garlic mayo sauce spread on the paneer make this worthy of a connoisseur's attention.

PREPARATION TIME : 20 MINUTES.   COOKING TIME : 6 TO 8 MINUTES.   MAKES 4 ROLLS.

To be mixed together into a marinade
1 cup fresh curds (*dahi*)
4 tsp ginger-garlic (*adrak-lehsun*) paste
1 tsp green chilli paste
1 tsp cornflour
1 tsp cumin seeds (*jeera*) powder
1 tsp white pepper powder
½ tsp cardamom (*elaichi*) powder
Salt to taste

For the *paneer tikkas*
16 pieces *paneer* (cottage cheese), cut into 25 mm. (1") cubes
16 pieces onions, cut into 25 mm. (1") cubes
16 pieces capsicum, cut into 25 mm. (1") cubes
1 tbsp oil for cooking

To be mixed into garlic mayo sauce
2 tsp ginger-garlic (*adrak-lehsun*) paste
2 pinches white pepper powder
8 tbsp mayonnaise

Other ingredients
2 cups shredded cabbage
Chaat masala to taste
4 spinach *rotis*, page 90
4 tbsp grated cheese

For the *paneer tikkas*
1. Combine the *paneer* cubes, onion cubes, capsicum cubes and half the marinade in a bowl and toss gently. Keep aside to marinate for 10 minutes.
2. On a satay stick, arrange 4 pieces each of *paneer*, capsicum and onion cubes alternatively. Repeat with the remaining ingredients to make 3 more satays.
3. Heat a non-stick *tava* (griddle) and cook the satays on a medium flame using oil till the *paneer* is light brown in colour from all the sides. Keep aside.

How to proceed
1. Combine the cabbage and *chaat masala* in a bowl, mix well and keep aside.
2. Place a spinach *roti* on a clean dry surface and slide the *paneer tikkas* from the satay stick in a row in the centre of the *roti*, gently using a knife.
3. Arrange ¼th of the cabbage mixture over the *tikkas*.
4. Finally spread ¼th of the remaining marinade, 2 tbsp of garlic mayo sauce and a tbsp of grated cheese over it and roll it up tightly.
5. Repeat with the remaining ingredients to make 3 more rolls.
6. Wrap a tissue paper around each roll and serve immediately.

~ Achaari Aloo Roll ~

Achaar is synonymous with Indian cuisine. Undoubtedly, it adds a brilliant touch to wraps too! Lacing the spicy potato filling with aam aur chane ka achaar makes your tongue tingle with joy. This recipe has to be planned in advance as the achaar has to be marinated for 3 to 4 days. Else, you can buy readymade aam ka achaar.

PREPARATION TIME : 20 MINUTES.   COOKING TIME : 20 MINUTES.   MAKES 4 ROLLS.

For the *aam aur chane ka achaar*
1½ cups grated raw mangoes *(kairi)*
1 tsp turmeric powder *(haldi)*
1 tbsp salt
1 tbsp fenugreek *(methi)* seeds
½ cup *kabuli chana* (chick peas*)*
1 tbsp fenugreek seeds *(methi)* powder
1 tbsp fennel seeds *(saunf)*
½ tsp asafoetida *(hing)*
1 tsp nigella seeds *(kalonji)*
14 whole dry Kashmiri red chillies
1 tbsp chilli powder
1¼ cups mustard oil

For the spicy potato filling
2 tbsp oil
1 tsp cumin seeds *(jeera)*
½ cup finely chopped onions
2 tsp finely chopped green chillies
1 tsp grated ginger *(adrak)*
1½ cups boiled, peeled and mashed potatoes
½ cup boiled green peas
2 tsp *chaat masala*
2 tsp *garam masala*
1 tbsp finely chopped coriander *(dhania)*
Salt to taste

Other ingredients
1 cup onion rings
Chaat masala to taste
4 *rotis*, page 90

For *aam aur chane ka achaar*
1. Combine the mangoes, turmeric powder and salt in a bowl, mix well and leave aside for 30 minutes. Squeeze out all the water from the mangoes and keep refrigerated till use.
2. Soak the *kabuli chana* and fenugreek seeds in the mango water overnight.
3. Combine the fenugreek seeds powder, fennel seeds, asafoetida, nigella seeds, whole red chillies, chilli powder, soaked *kabuli chana* mixture and grated mangoes in a bowl and mix well.
4. Heat the mustard oil in a small pan and cool completely. Add it to the prepared mixture.
5. Place the pickle in a sterilised glass jar and store it in a cool dry place.
6. The pickle is ready for use after 3 to 4 days.

For the spicy potato filling
1. Heat the oil in a *kadhai* and add the cumin seeds.
2. When the seeds crackle, add the onions and sauté on a medium flame till they turn translucent.
3. Add the green chillies and ginger and sauté on a medium flame for 30 seconds.
4. Add the potatoes, green peas, *chaat masala*, *garam masala*, coriander and salt, mix well and sauté on a medium flame for another 2 to 3 minutes. Keep aside.

How to proceed
1. Combine the onion rings and *chaat masala* in a bowl, mix well and keep aside.
2. Place a *roti* on a clean dry surface and arrange ¼th of the spicy potato filling in a row in the centre of the *roti*.
3. Spread 1 tsp of aam aur chane ka achaar and ¼ cup of onion rings over it and roll it up tightly.
4. Repeat with the remaining ingredients to make 3 more rolls.
5. Wrap a tissue paper around each roll and serve immediately.

~International Wraps & Rolls~

Let your taste buds travel around the globe, with these delectable international recipes! Influenced by various cuisines of the East as well as the West, we have conjured up some lip-smacking wraps that combine the best of the two worlds. Nonetheless, some delights are best made the authentic way – and so, we've retained some original recipes such as the *Burritos,* **page 36,** as it is.

All those who enjoy having spicy Thai food will be overjoyed when they sample the delicious *Thai Satay Paneer Wrap,* **page 56.** Die-hard Chinese cuisine fans will definitely not be disappointed when they try out the wide range of rolls such as the *Vegetable Manchurian Roll,* **page 38,** *Vegetable and Noodle Wrap,* **page 40** and the *Mushroom Schezuan Wrap,* **page 48.**

Your guests are sure to be impressed by your culinary skills when they bite into exotic wraps like the *Mexican Tortilla Wrap,* **page 42,** the *Lebanese Roll,* **page 50** and the *Potato Cream Cheese Roll,* **page 58.** What makes these wraps special is the use of wonderful ingredients like olives, baby corn, asparagus and refried beans.

Those with an adventurous spirit can go for recipes such as the *Herbed Cottage Cheese Wrap,* **page 44** and the *Chilli Paneer Wrap,* **page 60.** The beauty of these amazing rolls is that one need not stick to the recipes as they are. You can mix and match sauces and fillings from different recipes and create wraps of your own.

≈ Burrítos ≈

Straight from the kitchens of Mexico, burrito is the first thing that comes to our mind when we think of international wraps. The combination of guacamole, refried beans and oodles of cheese makes this traditional wrap truly irresistible.

PREPARATION TIME : 25 MINUTES.   COOKING TIME : 10 TO 12 MINUTES.   MAKES 4 BURRITOS.

For the guacamole
¾ cup ripe avocado pulp
1 tsp lemon juice
¼ cup finely chopped onions
¼ cup finely chopped tomatoes
1 tsp finely chopped green chillies
1 tsp finely chopped garlic *(lehsun)*
Salt to taste

For the refried beans
1½ tsp oil
1 tbsp finely chopped garlic *(lehsun)*
½ cup finely chopped onions
1 cup finely chopped tomatoes
¼ cup finely chopped capsicum
1 cup soaked, cooked and drained *rajma* (kidney beans)
1 tsp chilli powder
1 tsp roasted cumin seeds *(jeera)* powder
Salt to taste

Other Ingredients
4 tortillas, page 90
1 cup finely chopped tomatoes
1 cup finely chopped spring onions
8 tbsp sour cream, page 94
8 tbsp grated processed cheese
4 tbsp crushed corn chips

For the guacamole
Combine all the ingredients in a bowl and mash well using a fork and refrigerate for at least an hour. Keep aside.

For the refried beans
1. Heat the oil in a deep pan, add the garlic and onions and sauté till the onions turn translucent.
2. Add the tomatoes and sauté for another 3 to 4 minutes.
3. Add the capsicum, *rajma*, chilli powder; cumin seeds powder and salt, mix well and cook for 5 minutes or till the mixture is dry and keep aside.

How to proceed
1. Place a tortilla on a clean dry surface and arrange ¼th of the refried beans in a row in the centre of the *roti*.
2. Arrange ¼ cup each of tomatoes and spring onions over it.
3. Spread ¼th of the guacamole and 2 tbsp of sour cream over it.
4. Finally sprinkle 2 tbsp of cheese and 1 tbsp of corn chips over it and roll it up tightly.
5. Repeat with the remaining ingredients to make 3 more burritos.
6. Wrap a tissue paper around each burrito and serve immediately.

~ Vegetable Manchurian Roll ~

These rolls adds an all-new dimension to the simple Manchurian. Serve it with the lovely sweet and sour sauce, Schezuan sauce and salads to experience a unique mélange of flavours. Of course, don't forget the stir-fried rice to complete the Chinese experience.

PREPARATION TIME : 15 MINUTES.   COOKING TIME : 20 MINUTES.   MAKES 4 ROLLS.

For the vegetable balls
2 cups finely chopped cabbage
¼ cup grated carrots
⅓ cup finely chopped spring onions
¼ cup cornflour
2 tsp finely chopped garlic (lehsun)
1 tsp finely chopped green chillies
¼ tsp MSG (Mono sodium glutamate), optional
Salt and white pepper powder to taste
Oil for deep-frying

For the Manchurian sauce
2 tbsp oil
1 tsp finely chopped garlic (lehsun)
2 tsp finely chopped green chillies
2 tsp finely chopped ginger (adrak)
2 tsp dark soya sauce
2 tbsp cornflour dissolved in ½ cup water
2 pinches sugar
Salt to taste

Other ingredients
4 rotis, page 90
1 cup stir-fried rice, page 95
1 cup shredded cabbage
6 tbsp Schezuan sauce, page 93
2 tbsp sweet and sour sauce, page 92

For the vegetable balls
1. Combine all the ingredients, except the oil, in a bowl and mix well.
2. Divide the mixture into 16 equal portions and shape each portion into a round ball.

3. Heat the oil in a *kadhai* and deep-fry the balls on a medium flame till they are golden brown in colour from all sides. Drain on absorbent paper and keep aside.

For the Manchurian sauce
1. Heat the oil in a wok or frying pan over a high flame.
2. Add the garlic, green chillies and ginger and stir-fry on a high flame for a few seconds.
3. Add ½ cup of water, soya sauce, cornflour paste, sugar and salt, mix well and simmer for a few minutes till the sauce thickens, while stirring continuously. Keep aside.

How to proceed
1. Just before serving, put the vegetable balls in the sauce and bring to boil.
2. Place the *roti* on a clean dry surface and arrange ¼th of the stir-fried rice in a row in the centre of the *roti*.
3. Arrange 4 vegetable balls and ¼ cup of cabbage over it.
4. Finally spread 1½ tbsp of Schezuan sauce and ½ tbsp of sweet and sour sauce over it and roll it up tightly.
5. Repeat with the remaining ingredients to make 3 more rolls.
6. Wrap a tissue paper around each roll and serve immediately.

Handy tip: Make the rolls immediately once the vegetable balls have been boiled with the Manchurian sauce to prevent the sauce from drying up and becoming gelatinous.

~ Mexican Tortilla Wrap ~

This wholesome wrap can be relished as a complete meal. A delectable fusion of cheesy pepper rice and refried beans pepped up with green garlic sauce makes this must-try. Don't forget to add sour cream, which widens the range of flavours that play around in this wrap! When fresh green garlic is not in season, use half the quantity of dry garlic.

PREPARATION TIME : 15 MINUTES.   COOKING TIME : 5 TO 7 MINUTES.   MAKES 4 WRAPS.

For the cheesy pepper rice
3 tbsp oil
1 tbsp chilli-garlic *chutney*, page 93
2 tbsp finely chopped celery (*ajmoda*)
½ cup onion slices
3 tbsp capsicum strips
2 tsp dry red chilli flakes
4 tbsp grated processed cheese
Salt to taste
1 cup cooked rice, refer handy tip

To be mixed together into green garlic sauce
1 tbsp finely chopped coriander (*dhania*)
1 tsp finely chopped green chillies
2 tbsp finely chopped fresh green garlic (*hara lehsun*)
1 tsp lemon juice
1 tbsp powdered sugar
2 tsp white vinegar
Salt to taste

Other Ingredients
4 tortillas, page 90
1 recipe refried beans, page 36
4 tbsp finely chopped spring onion whites
4 tbsp sour cream, page 94

For the cheesy pepper rice
1. Heat the oil in a deep pan, add the chilli-garlic *chutney* and celery and sauté on a medium flame for few seconds.
2. Add the onions and capsicum and sauté on a high flame till the onions turn translucent.
3. Add the chilli flakes, cheese and salt and cook on a medium flame for a few seconds, while stirring continuously.
4. Add the rice, mix well and keep aside.

How to proceed
1. Place a tortilla on a clean dry surface and place ¼th of the cheesy pepper rice in a row in the centre of the tortilla.
2. Arrange ¼th of the refried beans and spread ¼th of the green garlic sauce over it.
3. Arrange 1 tbsp of spring onion whites and spread 1 tbsp of sour cream over it and roll it up tightly.
4. Repeat with the remaining ingredients to make 3 more wraps.
5. Wrap a tissue paper around each wrap and serve immediately.

Handy tip: For 1 cup of cooked rice, boil a vesselful of water with a little salt. Add ½ cup of raw rice and cook till done. Strain using a sieve and use as per the recipe.

≈ Herbed Cottage Cheese Wrap ≈

Fit to be called an international gourmet dish, although it is easy and non-fussy! What makes this wrap stand out from the rest is the exotic green mayonnaise flavoured with oregano, which gives the paneer a classic touch. Wrapping it with lettuce, carrots and sprouts adds crunch to it.

PREPARATION TIME : 10 MINUTES.   COOKING TIME : NIL.   MAKES 4 WRAPS.

For the green mayonnaise
½ cup finely chopped coriander *(dhania)*
¼ cup chopped parsley
2 tsp finely chopped green chillies
2 tbsp finely chopped pickled onions, refer handy tip
1 tsp lemon juice
A pinch sugar
Salt to taste
½ cup mayonnaise

Other Ingredients
1 cup *paneer* (cottage cheese), cut into 10 mm. (1 cm.) x 10 mm. (1 cm.) pieces
½ tsp dry red chilli flakes
¼ tsp oregano
Salt to taste
4 spinach *rotis*, page 90
2 cups roughly torn lettuce
1 cup bean sprouts
1 cup grated carrots

For the green mayonnaise
1. Combine the coriander, parsley, green chillies, pickled onions, lemon juice, sugar and salt and blend in a mixer to a smooth paste.
2. Transfer it to a bowl, add the mayonnaise, mix well and refrigerate for an hour.

How to proceed
1. Combine the *paneer*, chilli flakes, oregano and salt in a bowl, mix well and keep aside.
2. Place a spinach *roti* on a clean dry surface and arrange ½ cup of lettuce in a row in the centre of the *roti*.
3. Arrange ¼th of the herbed *paneer* mixture and ¼ cup each of bean sprouts and carrots over it.
4. Finally spread ¼th of the green mayonnaise over it and roll it up tightly.
5. Repeat with the remaining ingredients to make 3 more wraps.
6. Wrap a tissue paper around each wrap and serve immediately.

Handy tip: Pickled onions are baby onions, usually preserved in salted water. They are available in select food stores.

≈ Cheese Corn Balls Wrap ≈

It's all about the ingredients, honey! Get them right, and you'd have crossed half the bridge. It's the wise selection of ingredients that makes this wrap special. The cheesy flavour of cheese corn balls topped with tangy salsa and crunchy corn chips will be enjoyed by all.

PREPARATION TIME : 15 MINUTES.   COOKING TIME : 20 MINUTES.   MAKES 4 WRAPS.

For the cheese corn balls

2 tbsp butter
2½ tbsp plain flour (maida)
½ cup warm milk
¾ cup boiled and crushed sweet corn kernels (makai ke dane)
2 tsp finely chopped green chillies
⅓ cup grated cheese
Salt to taste
Breadcrumbs for coating
Oil for deep-frying

For the cooked salsa

2 tsp oil
2 tsp garlic (lehsun) paste
2 tsp green chilli paste
½ cup finely chopped spring onions whites
½ cup finely chopped capsicum
1 cup finely chopped tomatoes
½ tsp vinegar
½ tsp oregano
Salt to taste

Other Ingredients

4 rotis, page 90
2 cups roughly torn lettuce
8 tbsp crushed corn chips

For the cheese corn balls

1. Heat the butter in a deep non-stick pan, add the flour and cook for a minute.
2. Add the milk and allow to simmer till the mixture thickens and leaves the sides of the pan, while stirring continuously. Keep aside to cool.
3. Combine the crushed corn, green chillies, cheese and salt with the thickened milk mixture in a bowl and mix well.
4. Divide the mixture into 12 equal portions and shape each into a round ball.
5. Roll each ball in bread crumbs in such a way that the balls are evenly coated from all sides.
6. Heat the oil in a kadhai and deep-fry the balls on a medium flame till they are golden brown in colour from all sides. Drain on absorbent paper and keep aside.

For the cooked salsa

1. Heat the oil in a deep pan, add the garlic paste, green chilli paste, spring onion whites and capsicum and sauté on a medium flame till the spring onions turn translucent.
2. Add the tomatoes, vinegar, oregano and salt, mix gently and cook on a medium flame for 2 to 3 minutes, while stirring continuously. Keep aside.

How to proceed

1. Place a roti on a clean dry surface and arrange ½ cup of lettuce in a row in the centre of the roti.
2. Arrange 3 cheese corn balls over it.
3. Arrange ¼th of the cooked salsa and sprinkle 2 tbsp of crushed corn chips over it and roll it up tightly.
4. Repeat with the remaining ingredients to make 3 more wraps.
5. Wrap a tissue paper around each wrap and serve immediately.

≈ Lebanese Roll ≈

Feel the soul of Lebanon with this scrumptious wrap prepared with chick pea based hummus, parsley hinted felafel and sesame seeds based tahini. Adding jalapeno peppers and chilli flakes, makes this wrap really spicy too!

PREPARATION TIME : 20 MINUTES.   COOKING TIME : 15 TO 20 MINUTES.   MAKES 4 ROLLS.

For the *felafel*
1 cup *kabuli chana* (chick peas), soaked overnight
¼ cup chopped coriander *(dhania)*
¼ cup finely chopped parsley
½ cup mint leaves *(phudina)*
1 tsp finely chopped green chillies
2 tsp finely chopped garlic *(lehsun)*
½ tsp roasted cumin seeds *(jeera)* powder
Salt to taste
Oil for deep-frying

To be ground together for the hummus
1 cup boiled *kabuli chana* (chick peas)
2 tsp chopped garlic *(lehsun)*
2 tsp lemon juice
4 tbsp fresh curds *(dahi)*
Salt to taste
1 tsp chilli powder
1 tbsp finely chopped parsley
3 tbsp oil
2 to 3 tbsp water

For the *tahini*
¾ cup sesame seeds *(til)*, roasted
¼ cup *chana dal* (split Bengal gram), roasted
1 tbsp vinegar
4 tbsp fresh curds *(dahi)*
2 tsp garlic *(lehsun)*
1 tsp oil
1 tsp chilli powder
1 tsp cumin seeds *(jeera)* powder
Salt to taste

Other ingredients
4 *rotis*, page 90

2 cups roughly torn lettuce
4 tbsp pickled jalapenos rings
1 tsp dry red chilli flakes

For the *felafel*
1. Combine all the ingredients, except the oil, and blend in a mixer to a coarse paste without using any water.
2. Divide the mixture into 20 equal portions and shape each portion into a round ball.
3. Heat the oil in a *kadhai* and deep-fry the *felafels* over a medium flame till they are golden brown in colour from all sides.
4. Drain on absorbent paper and keep aside.

For the *tahini*
1. Combine the sesame seeds and *chana dal* and blend in a mixer to a fine powder.
2. Transfer the powder to a bowl, add all the remaining ingredients and mix well. Keep aside.

How to proceed
1. Place a *roti* on a clean dry surface and spread ¼th of the hummus evenly over it.
2. Place ½ cup of lettuce in a row in the centre of the *roti*.
3. Place 5 *felafels* over the lettuce and spread ¼th of the *tahini* over it.
4. Arrange 1 tbsp of jalapeno rings and sprinkle ¼ tsp of chilli flakes over it and roll it up tightly.
5. Repeat with the remaining ingredients to make 3 more rolls.
6. Wrap a tissue paper around each roll and serve immediately.

~ Asparagus and Baby Corn Wrap ~

Bite into this delightful wrap prepared with exotic ingredients like asparagus and baby corn flavoured with oregano and chilli flakes, and forget yourself in the medley of flavours that challenge the exquisite cheese sauce! Top it with lettuce, carrots and bean sprouts to add a nice crispy texture.

PREPARATION TIME : 10 MINUTES.   COOKING TIME : 7 TO 8 MINUTES.   MAKES 4 WRAPS.

For the asparagus-baby corn stir-fry
1 tbsp butter
1¼ cups asparagus, cut into 20 mm. (2 cm.) pieces and blanched
8 to 10 nos. baby corn, cut into 20 mm. (2 cm.) pieces and blanched
¼ cup sweet corn kernels (*makai ke dane*)
2 tsp dry red chilli flakes
1 tsp oregano
Salt to taste

For the cheese sauce
2 tbsp butter
½ tbsp finely chopped garlic (*lehsun*)
¼ cup milk
⅓ cup grated cheese
½ tsp oregano
¼ cup cream
1 tsp dry red chilli flakes
Salt to taste

Other Ingredients
8 tbsp grated carrots
4 tbsp bean sprouts
Salt to taste
4 spinach *rotis*, page 90
1 cup roughly torn lettuce

For the asparagus-baby corn stir-fry
Heat the butter in a deep non-stick pan, add the asparagus, baby corn, corn, chilli flakes, oregano and salt and sauté over a high flame for 2 to 3 minutes. Keep aside.

For the cheese sauce
1. Heat the butter in a broad non-stick pan, add the garlic and sauté for a few seconds.
2. Add the milk, cheese, oregano, cream, chilli flakes and salt and stir over a slow flame till the cheese melts completely and the sauce thickens. Keep aside.

How to proceed
1. Combine the carrots, bean sprouts and salt in a bowl, mix well and keep aside.
2. Place a spinach *roti* on a clean dry surface and arrange ¼ cup of lettuce in a row in the centre of the *roti*.
3. Arrange ¼th of the asparagus-baby corn stir-fry and ¼th of the carrot-bean sprouts mixture over it.
4. Finally spread ¼th of the cheese sauce over it and roll it up tightly.
5. Repeat with the remaining ingredients to make 3 more wraps.
6. Wrap a tissue paper around each wrap and serve immediately.

～ Mexican Kebab Roll ～

Punjab meets Mexico in this innovative roll, where the simple paneer tikkas have been given a Mexican touch by adding cocoa to the marinade! Finish by adding sour cream, to add a lovely tangy taste to the roll. The interplay of flavours in this roll makes it unforgettable.

PREPARATION TIME : 10 MINUTES.   COOKING TIME : 6 TO 8 MINUTES.   MAKES 4 ROLLS.

To be mixed into a marinade

2 tsp cocoa powder
2 tsp chilli powder
2 tbsp fresh thick curds *(dahi)*
4 tsp finely chopped garlic *(lehsun)*
1 tbsp cornflour
1 tsp oregano
3 tbsp oil
Salt and freshly ground pepper to taste

For the Mexican *kebabs*

8 pieces *paneer* (cottage cheese), cut into 25 mm. (1") cubes
8 pieces onions, cut into 25 mm. (1") cubes
8 pieces babycorn, cut into 25 mm. (1") cubes and blanched
8 pieces capsicum, cut into 25 mm. (1") cubes
8 pieces mushroom *(khumbh),* blanched
1 tbsp oil for cooking

Other Ingredients

4 *rotis*, page 90 or tortillas, page 90
1 recipe sour cream, page 94
1 cup finely chopped spring onions
1 tsp dry red chilli flakes

For the Mexican *kebabs*

1. Combine the *paneer* cubes, onion cubes, babycorn, capsicum cubes, mushrooms and half the marinade in a bowl and toss gently. Keep aside to marinate for 10 minutes.
2. On a satay stick, arrange 2 pieces each of *paneer* cubes, onion cubes, babycorn, capsicum cubes and mushrooms. Repeat with the remaining ingredients to make 3 more satays.
3. Heat a non-stick *tava* (griddle) and cook the satays on a medium flame using oil till the vegetables turn light brown in colour from all the sides. Keep aside.

How to proceed

1. Place a *roti* on a clean dry surface and spread ¼th of the sour cream over it.
2. Slide the Mexican *kebabs* from 1 satay stick in a row in the centre of the *roti*, gently using a knife.
3. Arrange ¼ cup of spring onions and sprinkle ¼ tsp of chilli flakes over it.
4. Finally spread ¼th of the remaining marinade over it and roll it up tightly.
5. Repeat with the remaining ingredients to make 3 more rolls.
6. Wrap a tissue paper around each roll and serve immediately.

⁓ Potato Cream Cheese Roll ⁓

I've given a nice Mediterranean feel to the humble potato, by lining it with olive cream cheese sauce. The spiced mayonnaise boosts the taste of this wrap, which becomes all the more exotic by the addition of veggies like baby corn and lettuce!

PREPARATION TIME : 20 MINUTES.   COOKING TIME : 4 TO 5 MINUTES.   MAKES 4 ROLLS.

For the potato wedge mixture
1 tbsp butter
2 cups peeled and parboiled potato wedges
½ cup capsicum strips
½ cup blanched baby corn strips
1 tsp dry red chilli flakes
½ tsp oregano
Salt to taste

For the olive cream cheese sauce
½ cup grated *paneer* (cottage cheese)
1 tbsp fresh cream
2 tbsp cheese spread
6 to 8 black olives, deseeded and chopped
1 tbsp chopped celery (*ajmoda*)
Salt to taste

To be mixed together into a spiced mayonnaise
½ cup mayonnaise
2 tsp tomato ketchup
4 tbsp finely chopped onions
2 tsp finely chopped green chillies
½ tsp mustard powder
3 tbsp milk
Salt to taste

Other ingredients
1 cup grated carrots
Salt to taste
4 spinach *rotis*, page 90
2 cups roughly torn lettuce

For the potato wedge mixture
1. Heat the butter in a broad non-stick pan, add the potatoes and sauté on a medium flame for 2 to 3 minutes or till the sides turn golden brown in colour from all sides.
2. Add the capsicum and sauté on a medium flame for another minute.
3. Add baby corn, chilli flakes, oregano and salt and sauté for another minute. Keep aside.

For the olive cream cheese sauce
1. Combine the *paneer*, fresh cream and cheese spread in a bowl and mix well till it is smooth and creamy.
2. Add all the remaining ingredients, mix well and refrigerate for at least an hour.

How to proceed
1. Combine the carrots and salt in a bowl, mix well and keep aside.
2. Place a spinach *roti* on a clean dry surface and arrange ½ cup of lettuce in a row in the centre on the *roti*.
3. Spread ¼th of the olive cream cheese sauce over the lettuce.
4. Arrange ¼th of the potato wedge mixture and ¼th of the carrots over it.
5. Finally spread ¼th of the spiced mayonnaise over it and roll it up tightly.
6. Repeat with the remaining ingredients to make 3 more rolls.
7. Wrap a tissue paper around each roll and serve immediately.

≈ Chilli Paneer Wrap ≈

Perk up the ever-popular chilli paneer with rice and stir-fried vegetables prepared in Oriental style. The spiciness is enhanced by lacing it with sweet and sour sauce. Though elaborate, the experience is definitely worth the effort!

Its only the prep time which is more.... The cooking time is very minimal. So finish your pre-preps and leave the actual cooking and assorting when guests arrive as making the chilli paneer too much in advance might render them chewy.

PREPARATION TIME : 20 MINUTES.   COOKING TIME : 15 MINUTES.   MAKES 4 WRAPS.

For the chilli *paneer*
¼ cup cornflour
¼ cup plain flour (*maida*)
1 tsp soya sauce
A pinch baking powder
Salt to taste
Oil for deep-frying
12 *paneer* (cottage cheese) pieces, cut into 38 mm.
(1½″) x 12 mm. (½″) strips
1 tbsp oil
1 tsp grated ginger (*adrak*)
2 tsp finely chopped garlic (*lehsun*)
3 tsp finely chopped celery (*ajmoda*)
¼ cup finely chopped spring onion whites
2 to 3 green chillies, cut into 25 mm. (1″) pieces
¼ cup capsicum strips
1 tsp soya sauce
1 tsp sugar
A pinch MSG (Mono Sodium Glutamate), optional
1 tbsp cornflour, dissolved in 3 tbsp water
Salt to taste

For the stir-fried vegetables
2 tbsp oil
1 tbsp finely chopped ginger (*adrak*)
2 tsp finely chopped garlic (*lehsun*)
¼ cup finely chopped spring onion whites
¼ cup carrot juliennes
¼ cup shredded cabbage
½ cup bean sprouts

4 tbsp Schezuan sauce, page 93
1 tbsp vinegar
A pinch MSG (Mono Sodium Glutamate), optional
Salt to taste
A pinch sugar
¼ cup finely chopped spring onion greens

Other Ingredients
4 *rotis*, page 90
4 tbsp sweet and sour sauce, page 92

For the chilli *paneer*
1. Combine the cornflour, plain flour, soya sauce, baking powder, salt and approx. ¼ cup of water in a bowl and mix well to make a smooth batter.
2. Heat the oil in a *kadhai* on a medium flame and dip the *paneer* pieces in the prepared batter and deep-fry till they are golden brown in colour from all sides. Drain on absorbent paper and keep aside.
3. Heat the oil in a deep pan, add the ginger, garlic, celery, spring onion whites and green chillies and sauté on a high flame for 2 minutes.
4. Add the capsicum and sauté on a high flame for a few more seconds.
5. Add the soya sauce, sugar, MSG, cornflour paste and salt, mix well and simmer for a minute, while stirring continuously.
6. Add the fried *paneer,* toss well and cook on a medium flame for another minute. Keep aside.

For the stir-fried vegetables

1. Heat the oil in a wok or frying pan on a high flame, add the ginger and spring onion whites and sauté for 2 minutes.
2. Add all the remaining ingredients, except the spring onion greens, mix all and sauté on a high flame for another 3 minutes.
3. Add the spring onion greens, mix well and keep aside.

How to proceed

1. Place a *roti* on a clean dry surface and arrange a portion of the stir-fried vegetables in a row in the centre of the *roti*.
2. Arrange 3 chilli *paneer* pieces and spread 1 tbsp of sweet and sour sauce over it and roll it up tightly.
3. Repeat with the remaining ingredients to make 3 more wraps.
4. Wrap a tissue paper around each wrap and serve immediately.

~Healthy Wraps & Rolls~

Of course, we have not forgotten our health-conscious readers! Here is an entire section for those who wish to keep their waistline in check. The key to creating healthy wraps is to master the art of replacing high fat ingredients with their low-fat counterparts and choosing healthy methods of cooking.

All these wraps and rolls are not only low in calories as compared to the regular calorie laden wraps and rolls but are also a powerhouse of vital nutrients that keep our metabolism ticking. Some of the wraps viz. **Hara Bhara Tikki Roll, page 64, Chickpea and Soya Tikki Roll, page 68,** and **Mint and Masoor Roll, page 72,** are whipped up using *tikkis* that are shallow fried instead of deep-frying.

Some of the wraps have been prepared by simply stir-frying veggies that speed up the cooking and bring out a rush of aromas and flavours. Try out some of these wraps, like the **Mixed Sprouts Wrap, page 66,** and the **Makai Khumbh Jalfrazie Roll, page 78,** you'll definitely not feel as if it has been made in a low-fat fashion!. Enjoy the delectable rolls like **Herbed Yoghurt Corn Cake Wrap, page 82, Honeyed Tofu and Pepper Roll, page 84,** and the **Spinach Tahini Wrap, page 86,** and discover the magic of fusion cuisine in the comfort of your home, without compromising your health.

Eat these wraps as a part of the main meal or simply as a snack and watch yourself join the league of healthy people.

~ Mixed Sprouts Wrap ~

Sprouts can be boring or super interesting depending on how you make use of them! In this innovative recipe, I have spiced up the sprouts with a simple ginger-garlic paste and chilli powder. Another unique addition to the wrap is the amazing mint and low-fat curd dressing that refreshes you without piling on extra calories. Wrap them in soya rotis for an extra protein punch.

PREPARATION TIME : 15 MINUTES. COOKING TIME : 8 TO 10 MINUTES. MAKES 4 WRAPS.

For the sprouts stir-fry
2 tsp oil
2 tsp ginger-garlic (adrak-lehsun) paste
¾ cup finely chopped onions
1½ cups boiled mixed sprouts (chana, moong and matki)
½ cup boiled, peeled and mashed potatoes
½ tsp turmeric powder (haldi)
2 tsp chilli powder
¼ cup finely chopped coriander (dhania)
1 tsp lemon juice
Salt to taste

To be mixed together into a mint dressing
¾ cup low-fat curds (dahi), page 95
3 tbsp finely chopped mint leaves (phudina)
¼ tsp mustard (rai / sarson) powder
¼ tsp powdered sugar
Salt to taste

Other Ingredients
1 cup onion rings
Chaat masala to taste
4 soya rotis, page 90

For the sprouts stir-fry
1. Heat the oil in a deep non-stick pan, add the ginger-garlic paste and onions and sauté till the onions turn translucent. Sprinkle a little water to avoid the onions from burning.
2. Add the mixed sprouts, potatoes, turmeric powder and chilli powder, mix well and cook on a medium flame for 5 minutes, while stirring continuously.
3. Add the coriander, lemon juice and salt, mix well and keep aside to cool.

How to proceed
1. Combine the onion rings with chaat masala in a bowl, mix well and keep aside.
2. Place a soya roti on a clean dry surface and arrange ¼th of the sprouts stir-fry in a row in the centre of the roti.
3. Arrange ¼ cup of onion rings and ¼th of the mint dressing over it and roll it up tightly.
4. Repeat with the remaining ingredients to make 3 more wraps.
5. Wrap a tissue paper around each wrap and serve immediately.

≈ Chick Pea and Soya Tikki Roll ≈

The piece de resistance of this recipe is the chick pea soya tikkis. And you will be surprised to know that this delicious wrap is great for weight-watchers and heart patients. Soya helps lower cholesterol and the low-cal mayonnaise adds to the taste without scaring the calorie-counter!

PREPARATION TIME : 10 MINUTES.   COOKING TIME : 8 TO 10 MINUTES.   MAKES 4 ROLLS.
SOAKING TIME : 10 TO 15 MINUTES.

For the chick pea and soya *tikkis*
1 cup soya granules
1 cup boiled and drained *kabuli chana* (chick peas), refer handy tip
2 tbsp finely chopped mint leaves (*phudina*)
2 tsp chilli-garlic *chutney*, page 93
2 tsp finely chopped green chillies
2 tsp finely chopped ginger (*adrak*)
Salt to taste
1 tsp oil for cooking

Other ingredients
1 cup tomato slices
1 cup onion rings
2 tbsp finely chopped coriander (*dhania*)
Salt and freshly ground pepper to taste
4 *rotis*, page 90
8 tbsp low-cal mayonnaise, page 96

For the chick pea and soya *tikkis*
1. Soak the soya granules in hot water for 10 to 15 minutes. Drain and squeeze out all the water.
2. Combine the soya granules, *kabuli chana* and mint leaves and blend in a mixer to a coarse paste without using any water.
3. Add the chilli-garlic *chutney*, green chillies, ginger and salt and mix well.
4. Divide the mixture into 8 equal portions and shape each portion into a 50 mm. (2") oval flat *tikkis*.

5. Heat a non-stick *tava* (griddle) and cook each *tikki* on a medium flame using ⅛ tsp of oil till the *tikkis* turn golden brown in colour from both the sides. Keep aside.

How to proceed
1. Combine the tomatoes, onions, coriander, salt and pepper in a bowl and mix lightly and keep aside.
2. Place a *roti* on a clean dry surface and place 2 *tikkis* in a row in the centre of the *roti*.
3. Arrange ¼th of onion-tomato mixture and spread 2 tbsp of low-cal mayonnaise over it and roll it up tightly.
4. Repeat with the remaining ingredients to make 3 more rolls.
5. Wrap a tissue paper around each roll and serve immediately.

Hany tip: To get 1 cup of boiled *kabuli chana*, soak ½ cup *kabuli chana* overnight. Pressure cook till done, drain well and use as per the recipe.

Whole Wheat Salad Wrap

I love this one because it is simple and nutritious! This no-fuss wrap is rich in anti-oxidant rich veggies like tomatoes, spring onions, carrots, bean sprouts and lettuce that help reverse ageing. Not only is this wrap nutritious, it is also luscious due to presence of fresh herbs like coriander and mint. Wrap it up in a spinach roti for that fresh green look!

PREPARATION TIME : 15 MINUTES.   COOKING TIME : NIL.   MAKES 4 WRAPS.

For the salad
½ cup thinly sliced tomatoes
½ cup sliced spring onions
½ cup carrot, cut into thin strips
½ cup bean sprouts
1 cup shredded lettuce
2 tbsp finely chopped coriander *(dhania)*
2 tbsp finely chopped mint leaves *(phudina)*
½ tsp roasted cumin seeds *(jeera)* powder
½ tsp lemon juice
1 tsp olive oil or refined oil
Salt to taste

Other Ingredients
4 spinach *rotis*, page 90
8 tbsp garlic-tomato *chutney*, page 94
4 tbsp low-cal mayonnaise, page 96

For the salad
1. Combine the tomatoes, spring onions, carrots, bean sprouts, lettuce, coriander and mint leaves in a bowl and refrigerate for at least 30 minutes.
2. Just before making the wrap, add the cumin seeds powder, lemon juice, oil and salt to the vegetables, mix well and keep aside.

How to proceed
1. Place a spinach *roti* on a clean dry surface and spread 2 tbsp of the garlic-tomato *chutney* evenly over it.
2. Arrange ¼th of the salad and spread 1 tbsp of low-cal mayonnaise in a row in the centre of the *roti* and roll it up tightly.
3. Repeat with the remaining ingredients to make 3 more wraps.
4. Wrap a tissue paper around each wrap and serve immediately.

Paneer Khurchan Roll

Behold this yummy variation of egg bhurji! I've replaced egg with low-fat paneer and cooked it with assorted spices and veggies like tomatoes, spring onions and capsicum. The filling is therefore a powerhouse of vitamin C! Wrapping it with soya rotis makes it rich in folic acid and iron too.

PREPARATION TIME : 15 MINUTES.   COOKING TIME : 10 MINUTES.   MAKES 4 ROLLS.

For the *paneer khurchan* filling
2 tsp oil
1 tsp cumin seeds (*jeera*)
1 tbsp ginger-garlic (*adrak-lehsun*) paste
¾ cup finely chopped spring onion whites
½ cup finely chopped capsicum
½ cup tomato purée
½ tsp turmeric powder (*haldi*)
1 tsp chilli powder
2 tsp *chaat masala*
2 cups low-fat *paneer* (cottage cheese), page 96, cut into 10 mm. (1 cm.) cubes
Salt to taste
2 tbsp finely chopped coriander (*dhania*)

Other ingredients
1 cup onion rings
Chaat masala to taste
4 soya *rotis*, page 90
8 tsp healthy green *chutney*, page 92

For *paneer khurchan* filling
1. Heat the oil in a deep non-stick pan, and add the cumin seeds.
2. When the cumin seeds crackle, add the ginger-garlic paste and spring onion whites and sauté till the spring onions turn translucent. Sprinkle a little water to avoid the spring onions from burning.
3. Add the capsicum and cook on a medium flame for 2 to 3 minutes, wile stirring continuously.
4. Add the tomato purée, turmeric powder, chilli powder, *chaat masala*, *paneer*, salt and coriander and cook for another 2 minutes, while stirring continuously. Keep aside.

How to proceed
1. Combine the onion rings with *chaat masala* in a bowl, mix well and keep aside.
2. Place a *roti* on a clean dry surface and spread 2 tsp of healthy green *chutney* evenly over it.
3. Arrange ¼th of *paneer khurchan* filling in a row in the centre of the *roti*.
4. Arrange ¼ cup of onion rings over it and roll it up tightly.
5. Repeat with the remaining ingredients to make 3 more rolls.
6. Wrap a tissue paper around each roll and serve immediately.

≈ Stir-Fry Wrap ≈

Find heaven in Italy, and bring it back to your kitchen! This Italian-style wrap is prepared from exotic veggies like sweet corn, asparagus, baby corn and broccoli laced with a lovely tomato sauce. Top it with low-cal mayonnaise and roll it up in spinach rotis.

PREPARATION TIME : 15 MINUTES.   COOKING TIME : 15 MINUTES.   MAKES 4 WRAPS.

For the tomato sauce (makes ½ cup)
1 tsp olive oil or refined oil
½ tbsp finely chopped garlic *(lehsun)*
½ cup finely chopped onions
½ cup tomato purée
½ tsp white pepper powder
½ tsp oregano
1 bayleaf *(tejpatta)*
1 tsp sugar
½ tbsp finely chopped basil leaves
2 tsp low-fat butter
1 tbsp tomato ketchup
Salt to taste

For the stir-fried vegetables
1 tsp oil
½ cup boiled sweet corn kernels *(makai ke dane)*
½ cup blanched asparagus
½ cup baby corn, blanched and cut lengthwise
½ cup blanched broccoli florets
½ tsp oregano
½ tsp dry red chilli flakes
Salt to taste

Other ingredients
4 spinach *rotis*, page 90
4 tbsp low-cal mayonnaise, page 96

For the tomato sauce
1. Heat the oil in a broad non-stick pan, add the garlic and sauté on a medium flame for few seconds.
2. Add the onions and sauté till they turn translucent. Sprinkle a little water to avoid the onions from burning.
3. Add the tomato purée, bring to boil and simmer for 5 minutes or till the sauce thickens, while stirring continuously.
4. Add all the remaining ingredients and simmer for another 2 minutes, while stirring occasionally.
5. Discard the bayleaf and keep aside to cool.

For the stir-fried vegetables
1. Heat the oil in a deep non-stick pan, add all the vegetables and sauté on a medium flame for 2 minutes.
2. Add the oregano, chilli flakes and salt and cook on a medium flame for a minute, while stirring continuously. Keep aside.

How to proceed
1. Place a spinach *roti* on a clean dry surface and spread ¼th of the tomato sauce evenly over it.
2. Arrange ¼th of the stir-fried vegetables in a row in the centre of the *roti*.
3. Spread 1 tbsp of low-cal mayonnaise over it and roll it up tightly.
4. Repeat with the remaining ingredients to make 3 more wraps.
5. Wrap a tissue paper around each wrap and serve immediately.

Makai Khumbh Jalfrazie Roll

Punjabi cuisine is tempting and scary at the same time, thanks to the use of rich (fatty) ingredients! This tongue-tickling roll lets you enjoy the goodness of a Punjabi subzi without piling on extra pounds. It's a fantastic combination of capsicum, mushrooms, sweet corn and paneer, featuring a balance of flavours from sweet to spicy. It's also a powerhouse of antioxidants that help prevent heart-related ailments.

PREPARATION TIME : 15 MINUTES.   COOKING TIME : 6 TO 8 MINUTES.   MAKES 4 ROLLS.

For the *jalfrazie* filling

1 tbsp oil
½ cup onions slices
½ cup sliced capsicum
1 cup mushrooms *(khumbh),* cut into quarters
¼ tsp turmeric powder *(haldi)*
1 tsp chilli powder
½ tsp coriander-cumin seeds *(dhania-jeera)* powder
½ cup sliced tomatoes
3 tbsp tomato ketchup
¼ cup tomato purée
Salt to taste
1 cup low-fat *paneer* (cottage cheese), page 96, cut into 12 mm. (½") cubes
½ cup boiled sweet corn kernels *(makai ke dane)*
2 tsp vinegar
½ tsp *garam masala*
¼ tsp sugar
2 tbsp finely chopped coriander *(dhania)*

Other Ingredients

1 cup onion rings
Chaat masala to taste
4 *rotis*, page 90
4 tbsp garlic-tomato *chutney*, page 94

For the *jalfrazie* filling

1. Heat the oil in a deep non-stick pan, add the onions and capsicum and sauté on a medium flame for 2 minutes. Sprinkle a little water to avoid the spring onions and capsicum from burning.
2. Add the mushrooms, turmeric powder, chilli powder, coriander-cumin·seeds powder, tomatoes, tomato ketchup, tomato purée and salt and sauté on a slow flame for 4 to 5 minutes.
3. Add the *paneer*, sweet corn kernels, vinegar, *garam masala*, sugar and coriander and toss lightly. Keep aside.

How to proceed

1. Combine the onion rings with the *chaat masala* in a bowl, mix well and keep aside.
2. Place a *roti* on a clean dry surface and spread 1 tbsp of the garlic-tomato *chutney* evenly over it.
3. Arrange ¼th of the *jalfrazie* filling in a row in the centre of the *roti*.
4. Arrange ¼th of onion rings over it and roll it up tightly.
5. Repeat with the remaining ingredients to make 3 more rolls.
6. Wrap a tissue paper around each roll and serve immediately.

Herbed Yoghurt Corn Cake Wrap

I totally adore this wrap because of its unmistakable Thai influence! The lovely corn cakes, flavoured with lemon grass based red paste, tastes magical with fresh green garlic sauce. The magic is enhanced by lining the cakes with a blend of dill and yoghurt!

PREPARATION TIME : 20 MINUTES.   COOKING TIME : 8 TO 10 MINUTES.   MAKES 4 WRAPS.

To be ground together for the red curry paste

5 whole dry Kashmiri red chillies, soaked in warm water for 10 minutes and drained

¼ cup chopped onions

2 tbsp finely chopped garlic (lehsun)

1 tbsp grated ginger (adrak)

2 tbsp chopped lemon grass (hare chai ki patti)

3 tbsp chopped coriander (dhania)

½ tbsp coriander (dhania) powder

1 tbsp cumin seeds (jeera) powder

½ tsp white pepper

Salt to taste

For the corn cakes

2 cups boiled sweet corn kernels (makai ke dane), lightly crushed

2 tbsp red curry paste, recipe above

1 tbsp soya sauce

⅓ cup rice flour (chawal ka atta)

Salt to taste

Whole wheat bread crumbs for coating

1 tsp oil for cooking

To be mixed together for the green garlic sauce

1 tbsp finely chopped coriander (dhania)

1 tsp finely chopped green chillies

2 tbsp finely chopped fresh green garlic (hara lehsun)

1 tsp lemon juice

1 tbsp powdered sugar

2 tsp white vinegar

Salt to taste

Other Ingredients

1 cup grated carrots

Salt to taste

4 rotis, page 90

1 cup roughly torn lettuce

1 recipe yoghurt dill blend, page 72

For the corn cakes

1. Combine all the ingredients in a bowl and mix well.
2. Divide the mixture into 8 equal portions and shape each portion into a 50 mm. (2") oval flat cake.
3. Roll the cakes in bread crumbs so they are evenly coated from all the sides.
4. Heat the oil on a non-stick tava (griddle) and cook each cake, using ⅛ tsp of oil, till they are golden brown in colour from both the sides.
5. Drain on absorbent paper and keep aside.

How to proceed

1. Combine the carrots and salt in a bowl, mix well and keep aside.
2. Place a roti on a clean dry surface and arrange ¼ cup of lettuce in a row in the centre of the roti.
3. Place 2 corn cakes and spread ¼th of the green garlic sauce over it.
4. Spread ¼th of the yoghurt dill blend over it.
5. Finally arrange ¼th of the carrots over it and roll it up tightly.
6. Repeat with the remaining ingredients to make 3 more wraps.
7. Wrap a tissue paper around each wrap and serve immediately.

Honeyed Tofu and Pepper Roll

Roll a la Mediterranean! The specialty of this wrap is that it retains the original flavour of all the veggies. The secret ingredient that makes the recipe a sure-hit is the right use of honey marinated tofu to complement the smoky flavour of capsicum. So simple, and yet so fine, hope you enjoy this one as much as I enjoyed creating it!

PREPARATION TIME : 20 MINUTES.   COOKING TIME : 5 MINUTES.   MAKES 4 ROLLS.

For the lemon honey marinated tofu
1 tsp olive oil or refined oil
1 tsp honey
2 cloves garlic (*lehsun*), crushed
1 tsp lemon juice
2 pinches grated lemon rind
¼ tsp oregano
Salt and freshly ground pepper to taste
16 pieces tofu, cut into 25 mm. (1") cubes

For the herb marinated capsicum and baby corn
1 cup red capsicum, cut into quarters and deseeded
1 cup green capsicum, cut into quarters and deseeded
1 tsp olive oil or refined oil
2 tsp lemon juice
4 tsp finely chopped fresh basil
4 tsp finely chopped fresh parsley
Salt to taste
4 baby corn, cut into halves lengthwise and blanched

Other Ingredients
4 soya *rotis*, page 90
8 tbsp low-fat sour cream, page 94

For the lemon honey marinated tofu
1. Combine all the ingredients, except the tofu, in a bowl and mix well.
2. Add the tofu and toss well. Cover and refrigerate for at least an hour.

For the herb marinated capsicum and baby corn
1. Heat a non-stick *tava* (griddle), place the capsicum pieces on it with the skin side down and cook till the skin blisters and turns black.
2. Remove from the flame and keep aside covered with a damp kitchen towel for 5 minutes.
3. Peel away the skin and cut each capsicum piece into thick strips. Keep aside.
4. Combine the oil, lemon juice, basil, parsley and salt in a bowl and mix well.
5. Add the capsicum and baby corn, toss well and keep refrigerated to marinate for an hour.

How to proceed
1. Place a soya *roti* on a clean dry surface and place 4 lemon honey marinated tofu pieces in a row in the centre of the *roti*.
2. Arrange ¼th of the herb marinated capsicum and baby corn over the tofu.
3. Finally spread 2 tbsp of low-fat sour cream over it and roll it up tightly.
4. Repeat with the remaining ingredients to make 3 more rolls.
5. Wrap a tissue paper around each roll and serve immediately.

≈ Spinach Tahini Wrap ≈

This marvelous wrap is a delightful confluence of Indian and Middle Eastern cuisine. Tahini, a delectable sesame seed based sauce combines beautifully with the veggies cooked in an Indian manner. By rolling it in spinach rotis, the iron, calcium and fibre content has been increased substantially.

PREPARATION TIME : 15 MINUTES.   COOKING TIME : 5 TO 7 MINUTES.   MAKES 4 WRAPS.

For the filling

2 tsp oil
½ cup finely chopped onions
1 tsp finely chopped green chillies
1½ cups grated carrots
½ cup shredded cabbage
½ cup boiled, peeled and grated potatoes
2 tbsp chopped coriander (dhania)
Salt to taste

Other ingredients

4 spinach rotis, page 90
1 recipe tahini, page 50
1 recipe garlic-tomato chutney, page 94
1 cup roughly torn lettuce

For the filling

1. Heat the oil in a deep non-stick pan, add the onions and sauté till they turn translucent.
2. Add the green chillies, carrots, cabbage, potatoes, coriander and salt, mix well and sauté on a medium flame for 2 more minutes. Keep aside.

How to proceed

1. Place a spinach roti on a clean dry surface and spread ¼th of the tahini paste evenly over it.
2. Arrange ¼ cup of lettuce in a row in the centre of the roti.
3. Arrange ¼th of the filling and spread the garlic-tomato chutney over it and roll up tightly.
4. Repeat with the remaining ingredients to make 3 more wraps.
5. Wrap a tissue paper around each wrap and serve immediately.

~ Paneer Tikki Salsa Wrap ~

Rock and roll with this delectable fusion wrap that combines the utterly delicious paneer tikki with the yummy salsa! This wrap is so scrumptious that you'll not realise it is low-cal. I rolled up the tikki along with a handful of goodies like salads and low-cal mayonnaise to increase its health quotient.

PREPARATION TIME : 15 MINUTES. COOKING TIME : 8 TO 10 MINUTES. MAKES 4 WRAPS.

For the *paneer tikki*

1½ cups mashed low-fat *paneer* (cottage cheese), page 96
¾ cup boiled, peeled and mashed potatoes
2 tbsp chopped coriander (*dhania*)
1 tbsp green chilli paste
3 tbsp cornflour
Salt to taste
Whole wheat bread crumbs for rolling
1 tsp oil for cooking

Other ingredients

½ cup shredded cabbage
½ cup grated carrots
¾ cup sliced onions
Chaat masala to taste
4 spinach *rotis*, page 90
1 cup roughly torn lettuce
1 recipe cooked salsa, page 46
8 tbsp low-cal mayonnaise, page 96

For the *paneer tikkis*

1. Combine all the ingredients in a bowl and mix well.
2. Divide the mixture into 8 equal portions and shape each portion into a 50 mm. (2") oval flat *tikki*.
3. Roll each *tikki* in bread crumbs so that they evenly coated on all the sides.
4. Heat a non-stick *tava* (griddle) and cook each *tikki*, using ⅛ tsp of oil, on a medium flame till they are golden brown in colour from both the sides.
5. Drain on absorbent paper and keep aside.

How to proceed

1. Combine the cabbage, carrots, onions and *chaat masala* in a bowl, mix well and keep aside.
2. Place a spinach *roti* on a clean dry surface and arrange ¼th cup of lettuce in a row in the centre of the *roti*.
3. Place 2 *tikkis* and spread ¼th of the salsa evenly over it.
4. Arrange ¼th of the cabbage-carrot-onion mixture and spread 2 tbsp of mayonnaise over it and roll it up tightly.
5. Repeat with the remaining ingredients to make 3 more wraps.
6. Wrap a tissue paper around each wrap and serve immediately.

BASIC RECIPES

≈ Roti ≈

You need to be a tad patient to be able to roll
out the perfect roti, but it becomes quite easy
with practice! Roll out as thinly as possible
and spread it evenly over the hot wok/kadhai
to ensure that the roti is uniformly cooked.

PREPARATION TIME : A FEW MINUTES.
COOKING TIME : 7 TO 8 MINUTES.
MAKES 4 ROTIS.

---

1 cup whole wheat flour (*gehun ka atta*)
Salt to taste
1½ tbsp oil
Whole wheat flour (*gehun ka atta*) for rolling

1. Combine the flour, salt and 1 tbsp of oil in a bowl
   and knead into a soft dough using enough water.
   Keep aside for 15 minutes.
2. Knead again using the remaining ½ tbsp of oil till it
   is smooth and elastic.
3. Divide it into 4 equal portions and roll out each
   portion of the dough into a thin circle of 250 mm.
   (10") diameter using a little flour (Refer page 91,
   step 1).
4. Heat a wok / wide iron *kadhai* upside down on a
   high flame and when hot, place the *roti* gently
   over the wok / *kadhai* ensuring that no creases
   form on the surface (Refer page 91, step 2).
5. Cook it till small blisters appear on the surface.
   Turn over the *roti* and cook for few more seconds
   till done (Refer page 91, step 3).

6. Repeat with the remaining dough portions to
   make 3 more *rotis*.

VARIATIONS:

1. **Spinach Roti:** Add ¼ cup of spinach purée at step
   1 and proceed as per the recipe.
2. **Soya Roti:** Add 3 tbsp of soya flour at step 1 and
   proceed as per the recipe.

≈ Tortillas ≈

Any Mexican wrap will be incomplete without
these authentic tortillas.

PREPARATION TIME : 10 MINUTES.
COOKING TIME : 10 TO 12 MINUTES.
MAKES 4 TORTILLAS.

---

1 cup maize flour (*makai ka atta*)
¼ tsp chilli powder
¼ tsp carom seeds (*ajwain*), optional
2 tsp oil
Salt to taste
¼ tsp oil for kneading
Maize flour (*makai ka atta*) for rolling

1. Combine the maize flour, chilli powder, carom
   seeds, 1 tsp of oil and salt in a bowl and knead i n t o
   a soft dough adding hot water as required. Keep
   aside for 10 minutes.
2. Knead again using the remaining 1 tsp of oil till
   smooth and elastic

3. Divide it into 4 equal portions and roll out each portion of the dough between two sheets of plastic into a thin circle of 250 mm (10") diameter. Dust the tortilla generously with flour to make the rolling easier (Refer step 1).
4. Heat a wok / wide iron *kadhai* upside down on a high flame and when hot place the tortilla gently over the wok / *kadhai* ensuring that no creases form on the surface (Refer step 2).
5. Cook it till small blisters appear on the surface. Turn over the tortilla and cook for few more seconds till done (Refer step 3).
6. Repeat with the remaining dough portions to Make 3 more tortillas.

How to make a roti

How to make a wrap / roll

Place the filling in a single row in the centre of the *roti*.

Fold the two opposite ends of the *roti* over the stuffing.

Start rolling the *roti* from one open end over the 2 folded sides.

Roll the entire *roti* tightly and wrap a tissue paper around it.

≈ Sweet and Sour Sauce ≈

A tongue-tickler, this sauce teases your taste buds with its contrasting sweet and sour flavours. Try out our Vegetable Manchurian Roll, page 38, and Chilli Paneer Wrap, page 60, and with this fantastic sauce and watch your family drool over your culinary creations.

PREPARATION TIME : 5 MINUTES.
COOKING TIME : 10 TO 12 MINUTES.
MAKES APPROX. ¾ CUP.

¼ cup vinegar
1 tbsp tomato ketchup
¼ cup sugar
½ tbsp Schezuan sauce, page 93
1 tbsp cornflour, dissolved in 2 tbsp water
Salt to taste

1. Combine the vinegar, tomato ketchup, sugar, Schezuan sauce, cornflour paste and ¼ cup of water in a broad pan and simmer till the sauce thickens into pouring consistency, while stirring continuously. Keep aside to cool.
2. Add the salt, mix well and use as required.

≈ Healthy Green Chutney ≈

A mouth-watering chutney that elevates the taste of the Paneer Khurchan Roll, page 74, to a new level of excellence. Use it as a base for any roll or simply have it with a starter.

PREPARATION TIME : 10 MINUTES.
COOKING TIME : NIL.
MAKES 1 CUP (APPROX. 14 TBSP).

---

2 cups roughly chopped mint leaves (*phudina*)
1 cup roughly chopped coriander (*dhania*)
½ cup sliced onions
2 tsp lemon juice
1 tsp sugar
4 to 6 roughly chopped green chillies
Salt to taste

1. Combine all the ingredients and blend in a mixer to a smooth paste using water as required.
2. Keep refrigerated and use as required.

4. Add the vinegar and sugar, mix well and cook on a medium flame for another minute, while stirring continuously.
5. Keep refrigerated and use as required.

Handy tip : To make 1½ cups of red chilli paste, soak 35 to 40 whole dry red Kashmiri chillies in enough warm water for at least an hour. Drain the chillies, deseed them and blend in a mixer to a smooth paste adding enough water. Keep aside.

~Schezuan Sauce~

A treat for spice lovers! This amazing sauce is an essential part of Chinese cuisine. Try out the Vegetable and Noodle Wrap, page 40, and Mushroom Schezuan Wrap, page 48, to sample this sauce in different rolls. You can store this sauce in refrigerator and use when required.

PREPARATION TIME : 15 MINUTES.
COOKING TIME : 5 MINUTES.
MAKES APPROX. 3 CUPS.

½ cup oil
¼ tsp MSG (Mono sodium glutamate), optional
¼ cup finely chopped celery (ajmoda)
¼ cup finely chopped garlic (lehsun)
¼ cup finely chopped ginger (adrak)
½ cup tomato purée
1½ cups red chilli paste, refer handy tip
Salt to taste
2 tbsp vinegar
2 tsp sugar

1. Heat the oil in a kadhai till it smokes, add the MSG, celery, garlic and ginger, mix well and sauté on a medium flame for 30 seconds or till the flavour releases.
2. Add the tomato purée, mix well and cook on a medium flame for 2 minutes, while stirring continuously.
3. Add the red chilli paste, salt and 2 tbsp of water, mix well and simmer for a minute.

~ Chilli-Garlic Chutney ~

This easy-to-make chutney is ideal to perk up the flavour of any filling.

PREPARATION TIME : 5 MINUTES.
COOKING TIME : 5 MINUTES.
MAKES ½ CUP.
SOAKING TIME : 30 MINUTES.

---

16 whole dry Kashmiri red chillies, soaked in warm water for 30 minutes and drained
4 tbsp roughly chopped garlic (lehsun)
1 tbsp lemon juice
Salt to taste

1. Combine all the ingredients, along with 2 tbsp of water and blend in a mixer to a smooth paste.
2. Keep refrigerated and use as required.

≈ Sour Cream ≈

A great accompaniment to wraps with Mexican flavours, this dressing balances the taste in recipes like the Burritos, page 36, and Mexican Tortilla Wrap, page 42.

PREPARATION TIME : A FEW MINUTES.
COOKING TIME : NIL.
MAKES ¾ CUP (APPROX. 11 TBSP).

¾ cup cream, beaten lightly
2 tbsp lemon juice
Salt and freshly ground pepper to taste

1. Combine all the ingredients in a bowl and mix well.
2. Keep refrigerated and use as required.

VARIATION :
≈ Low-Fat Sour Cream ≈

Replace the cream with equal quantity of low-fat cream to make low-fat sour cream.

≈ Garlic-Tomato Chutney ≈

A unique twist has been given to the simple garlic chutney by adding tomatoes and spring onions to it. Tomato gives it the much needed tang, while the coriander and spring onion greens add to the crunch and earthy flavour. This chutney compliments Whole Wheat Salad Wrap, page 70, and Mint and Masoor Rolls, page 72.

PREPARATION TIME : 15 TO 20 MINUTES.
COOKING TIME : 10 MINUTES.
MAKES ¾ CUP (APPROX. 11 TBSP).
SOAKING TIME: 30 MINUTES.

3 whole dry Kashmiri red chillies, soaked in warm water for 30 minutes and drained
1 tsp olive oil or refined oil
¼ cup finely chopped spring onion whites
2 tbsp finely chopped garlic (lehsun)
Salt to taste
1 cup finely chopped tomatoes
1 tbsp finely chopped coriander (dhania)
1 tbsp tomato ketchup
1 tbsp finely chopped spring onion greens

1. Drain the soaked chillies and chop them finely.
2. Heat the oil in a broad non-stick pan, add the onions and garlic and sauté on a slow flame for 4 to 5 minutes till the onions turn translucent.

3. Add the chillies and salt and sauté on a slow flame for 30 seconds.
4. Add the tomatoes and 3 tbsp of water and cook for 12 to 15 minutes over a slow flame till the tomatoes are soft and all the water has evaporated. Mash lightly with the back of a spoon. Keep aside to cool.
5. Add the coriander, tomato ketchup and spring onion greens and mix well. Use as required.

Handy tip:

To keep the rice grains separate, cook the rice by boiling method, spread the cooked rice on tray and allow it to cool. Drizzle a little oil on the cooked rice, mix gently and keep aside till you require it.

≈ Stir-Fried Rice ≈

Oriental wraps taste amazing with this subtly-flavoured and aromatic rice. Spring onions add crunch whereas celery and garlic add the perfect zing to this delectable rice dish.

PREPARATION TIME : 10 MINUTES.
COOKING TIME : 15 MINUTES.
MAKES APPROX. 2 CUPS.

---

2 tbsp oil
1 tsp chopped garlic (lehsun)
1 tbsp finely chopped celery (ajmoda)
1 cup finely chopped spring onions
1½ cups cooked rice
Salt to taste

1. Heat the oil in a wok on a high flame, add the garlic, celery and spring onions and sauté for 2 minutes.
2. Add the cooked rice and salt and sauté on high flame for another 2 to 3 minutes. Use as required.

≈ Low-Fat Curds ≈

Low-fat curds are simple to make and a very good alternative to high-calorie curds. Use this to make yummy dressings, as I have done in Mixed Sprouts Wrap, page 66 and Mint and Masoor Roll, page 72.

PREPARATION TIME : NIL.
COOKING TIME : 30 SECONDS.
MAKES 5 CUPS.

---

1 litre low-fat milk (99.7% fat free, readily available in the market)
1 tbsp curds (dahi)

1. Warm the milk, add the curds and mix well.
2. Cover and keep aside to set (approx. 5 to 6 hours).
3. During the cold climate, place it inside a casserole or closed oven to set.

Variation : HUNG LOW-FAT CURDS
To get 1 cup of hung low-fat curds, tie 2 cups of low-fat curds in a cloth and hang it for ½ hour. Remove from the cloth and use as required.